MAKING SENSE OF BEHAVIOUR

UNDERSTANDING AND SUPPORTING
DEPRESSED CHILDREN AND YOUNG PEOPLE

by

Rob Long

A NASEN PUBLICATION

Published in 1999

© Rob Long

ISBN 1 901485 10 2

Published by NASEN.
NASEN is a company limited by guarantee, registered in England and Wales. Company No. 2674379.
NASEN is a registered charity. Charity No. 1007023.

Further copies of this book and details of NASEN's many other publications may be obtained from the Publications Department at its registered office: NASEN House, 4/5 Amber Business Village, Amber Close, Amington, Tamworth, Staffs. B77 4RP.
Tel: 01827 311500; Fax: 01827 313005
Email: welcome@nasen.org.uk; Website: www.nasen.org.uk

Cover design by Raphael Creative Design.
Typeset in Times by J. C. Typesetting and printed in the United Kingdom by Stowes (Stoke-on-Trent).

Contents

Preface

Understanding and Supporting Depressed Children and Young People is one of eight booklets in the series *Making Sense of Behaviour* by Rob Long. The others are *Exercising Self-control; Developing Self-esteem through Positive Entrapment for Pupils facing Emotional and Behavioural Difficulties; Friendships; Not Me, Miss! The Truth about Children who Lie; Challenging Confrontation: Information and Techniques for School Staff; Supporting Pupils with Emotional and Behavioural Difficulties through Consistency;* and *Learning to Wave: Some Everyday Guidelines for Stress Management.*

The first five titles give practical ideas and information for teachers to use with children with worrying behaviours in their classes. These are written to help teachers both understand and change some of the difficulties that children might experience (depression, lack of self-control, low self-esteem, friendship problems and lying).

Challenging Confrontation gives information and techniques for teachers to use when dealing with argumentative, angry and difficult pupils. *Supporting Pupils with Emotional and Behavioural Difficulties through Consistency* advocates a whole-school approach for low-level misbehaviours whilst *Learning to Wave* is written for teachers themselves. It contains advice about coping with the stress which might arise from dealing with children with behavioural problems.

Each book stands alone but when read as a set the behavioural issues and their solutions overlap and this emphasies the need for positive and consistent strategies to be put into place throughout the school.

Acknowledgements
The author and publishers wish to express their grateful thanks to Lorna Johnston, Agnes Donnelly and Dorothy Smith for their helpful suggestions and comments.

Understanding and Supporting Depressed Children and Young People

Introduction

While all children experience feelings of sadness, it is now recognised that children, and especially teenagers are prone to depression.

Some facts
- Some 2 in every 100 children under the age of 12 are depressed to the point of requiring specialist help and a further 4 to 5 in every 100 are on the edge of depression.
- 5 in every 100 teenagers are seriously depressed and twice that number are significantly distressed.
- In areas that face social deprivation, drugs and high crime etc the numbers are considerably higher.
- About 6 in every 100,000 15-19 year-old boys commit suicide each year in Britain and 1 or 2 per 100,000 girls of the same age commit suicide.
- The rates are lower for the 10-14 year-olds and suicide for the under-10 year-olds is extremely rare.
- In a secondary school of 1,000 pupils, about 50 students will be depressed in any year, while an inner city primary school of some 400 children could expect to have some 8 severely depressed children.

(Graham and Hughes, 1995)

Since many children suffering depression will turn their emotional difficulties in on themselves, they are often not a behavioural problem in class, and therefore may not receive the support they need. This booklet is aimed at providing information about depression and ideas for supporting children and young people who suffer it. Some consideration of children at risk of attempting suicide - the most extreme and tragic result to depression - will also be given. Furthermore it should be emphasised that while there are similarities between depression and the reactions children have during bereavement, bereavement is not covered by this booklet.

Many researchers believe that mood disorders - such as depression - in children and teenagers represent one of the most under-diagnosed illnesses of today.

When working with a depressed pupil it is essential to discuss concerns with other key people in school as well as making contact with both home and other agencies involved. Our aim in school is to offer appropriate and informed support to the pupil - not to act as a therapist.

What is depression?

Depression describes a much more negative emotion than just feeling "sad" or "fed up". It is often described as being like a fog descending in the mind, which drains effort and prevents decisions being made. Like most complicated moods there are many factors involved. During the adolescent years hormonal changes probably play a role - this helps explain why it is more common during the teenage years. But real events that can cause depression can occur at any age. If a child experiences a series of "sad" events then the conditions can exist for depression to develop.

Academic
- unexpectedly poor test results
- continued "poor" achievement compared to others

Relationships
- argument with a friend/s
- feeling different to rest of class

Loss
- loss of a favourite possession
- favourite relative moves away

Each of these events on their own would probably not result in depression. But when they occur in conjunction they can cause strong feelings of despair and feelings of helplessness and a lack of control. (Control is a core component of resiliency and self-esteem.) A final big event then happens and a child becomes trapped in the "pit" of depression. Once in this pit the depression will take on a force of its own. That is it seeks out more negative news and events to maintain itself. In other words when we become depressed and fall into the pit, instead of climbing out, we carry on digging.

Lack of control

We each have a sense of being in control of many events in our lives. We make choices and expect to succeed in steering ourselves through the demands of each day. Imagine how you would feel if you lost this, if you always expected to fail and the world seemed to control you despite your efforts. There are some children, and adults, who "learn to be helpless". Through their experiences they lose a sense of internal control. Their behaviour will appear flat, purposeless and depressed. It may be that at home they are in a large family. Perhaps everything is done for them. They fail to learn control. Some children will reflect this in the "I can't do it" response to every new challenge.

We can be at a loss sometimes to understand why some children underachieve in their work and lack personal confidence in new situations. These children have difficulties that would not merit referral to the Family Guidance Centre. They have negative emotions which act as a barrier to their learning. Learning requires confidence, the ability to "risk" failing. This booklet aims to provide a range of ideas and strategies to help support these children in school.

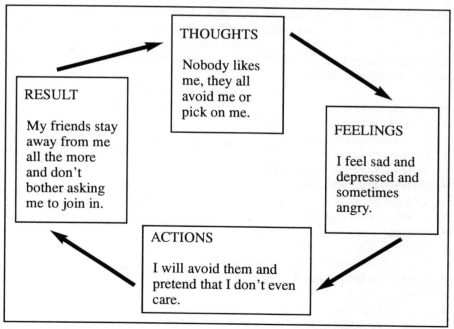

Self-Fulfilling Cycle of Negativity.

The pain of depression can be far worse than a physical pain. This internal pain of worthlessness and hopelessness can penetrate deep into a child's personality. They come to think poorly of themselves and will then act in ways that lead others to respond to them in a similar manner. As they experience rejections from people, the pupil feels worse and becomes more and more isolated. At such times it is not uncommon for depressed teenagers to engage in anti-social behaviour, and to become extremely hostile to people close to them. The internal logic is that they are creating in the minds of others the same negative attitudes and feelings they themselves are experiencing. Their depression will try to prevent them asking for help. Sometimes the only solution to their pain can tragically be suicide.

Signs of depression

Children experience essentially the same moods as adults but show different symptoms. They will often not have the vocabulary to explain what they are feeling and may therefore express their problems through their behaviour. The following signs can be seen as symptoms of depression just as a cough and runny nose are signs of a cold. Just as we do not need to know where we caught the cold to treat it, the same applies to depression. It's just like catching a "mental head cold". Some of the behavioural symptoms associated with depression include:

- sad expressions
- ill more often
- poor appetite or overeating
- poor concentration
- difficulty in making decisions
- feelings of hopelessness
- irritability
- emotionally volatile
- tearful
- frequent negative self-statements
- hate self and everything around them
- disruptive behaviour
- poor learning
- self-destructive
- poor peer relationships
- mood change - not a reaction to bereavement

Depression can be an indication of substance abuse.

When working with pupils who are passive and withdrawn:

- Reassure them that there is hope and that matters can improve.
- Avoid phrases such as, "come along and cheer up" or "It can't be that bad".
- Reassure them that you will stay with them.
- Be persistent in expressing your concerns about them.
- Be sensitive and guided by their response to physical contact, not every child always enjoys a cuddle.

Jane was 8 years old and had in a very short time faced several "little deaths". A best friend had moved away, her class teacher was on maternity leave and she was finding some of her work harder to manage.

You will need to be clear in the messages that you give to a depressed child. Children will often believe that they deserve to feel bad, that it is because they have done something so bad and that they are being punished. Older children may believe they are going crazy. We need to understand that depression is a trap that we can all fall into. The skill is in being able to get out of it. A key aim is to offer them definite practical help.

Depression can be understood and managed.

Confidentiality v need to know
This is clearly an important issue when we are working with children who need to feel they can trust the adult they are talking to. Much has been written about confidentiality in counselling. But in schools while we will be using counselling skills, we are not counsellors. Confidentiality refers to the professional responsibility of counsellors. Therefore if a pupil gives us information that suggests that they are in "real" danger, it is our responsibility to inform other relevant agencies. While we may feel that we are betraying a confidence the young person's safety must be paramount. Depression is a potentially life-threatening disorder. It can mask other intense feelings - anger, rage, hatred - and suicide can be an expression of such feelings. So referring on reflects our awareness that a child needs more specialist and intensive support as well as our concern for them.

What to say

These talks are private between you and me. I won't talk to other people about what we say. But if something is said which means you, or somebody else is in danger and needs help, then I will speak to those people who need to know, and can help. I will explain to you who I will see and why and stay with you throughout. (Use wording to suit your own style and understanding of the child.)

Pupils at suicide risk

The pain that children and young people feel comes in waves and then recedes. They may remain in pain but this is less severe. Therefore they can be seen and talked to within hours before they attempt suicide. There can even be an improvement in their mood as if the making of this final decision has lifted a great burden from them. Some of the recognised "at risk signs" include:

- Pupils who have already attempted suicide.
- Pupils whose parent or close relative committed suicide. (There is a risk of post-traumatic stress disorder which can increase the possibility of suicide.)
- Children with attention deficit disorder who will have experienced poor social relationships with peers can experience feelings of isolation, rejection and feelings of inadequacy. During adolescence this can coincide with them becoming self-centred and comparing themselves with others.
- Pupils involved with alcohol and/or substance abuse.
- Adolescents dealing with issues of sexuality. Research indicates that gay and lesbian teenagers attempt suicide at a rate of two to three times higher than their heterosexual peers.
- When a pupil's media idol dies or commits suicide it is not uncommon for vulnerable adolescents to copy.

Serious signs of depression

- marked change in personality
- dramatic and sudden decrease in school work
- verbal threats of suicide
- involvement in anti-social/delinquent behaviour
- no interest in appearance
- social isolation
- emotionally volatile
- discarding of prized possessions
- preoccupation with death
- possession of dangerous weapons eg knives
- sudden cheerfulness after prolonged depression

John was 15 and seemed to have lost all self-motivation. He no longer mixed with his friends. He stayed up late watching TV and slept in late. His appearance was unkempt and he was emotionally flat and generally lethargic.

When to refer on?

The *Code of Practice* (DfE, 1994) is intended to be a framework to help schools meet the needs of pupils with difficulties. After home, teachers and other support staff spend the most time with pupils and get to know them extremely well under a host of different circumstances. Most children who become depressed respond to positive care and support quite quickly.

If you have concerns as to whether your approach is suitable or whether the child requires more specialist help, refer on. Depression is a real risk factor for suicidal behaviour. Each week some two to three teenagers commit suicide and many thousands receive treatment over the year because of self-inflicted injury.

If in doubt, discuss your concerns with your head teacher, SENCO, school doctor or nurse, social worker, education welfare officer, educational psychologist.

> ## BE AWARE OF THE REACTION ERROR
> ## DON'T OVERREACT OR UNDERREACT

Offering support

There will be times when the pupil is reluctant to accept help. It can help to do the following activity in order to remind/teach the pupil that they have a big part to play in helping themselves (Hobday & Ollier, 1998).

Imagine you have been out walking and have slipped into a hole with steep sides. Draw a matchstick person at the bottom of the hole to represent you.

Family and friends come along to get you out of the hole. Draw some of the people at home and school who would be at the top of the hole.

What could they use to help you out? Yes, they could throw a rope down to you. Draw one in. What would you have to do for their efforts to help you work? Yes, you would need to take hold of the rope to enable them to pull you out.

So when help is offered, your task is to take hold of it. A bit like being ill in bed with a cold. You may be poorly, but you will be expected to take the medicine that is offered to help you.

This can show children their role in helping themselves. The nature of depression is that there will be many who need encouragement to take hold of the rope.

Key principles
We all know that we do not have direct control over how we feel. We cannot just "snap out of a bad feeling" but we can change what we think and what we do. And by doing this we can influence how we feel. Our efforts to help depressed children will be much easier if we always remember:

- Thoughts, feelings and behaviours each affect the other.
- Thoughts, feelings and actions are all linked to each other.

This is why whistling can sometimes lift our spirits. Have you ever tried to frown while whistling?

1. What we think will affect what we feel, and what we feel will affect what we think.
2. What we think will affect what we do, and what we do will affect what we think.
3. What we do will affect what we feel, and what we feel will affect what we do.

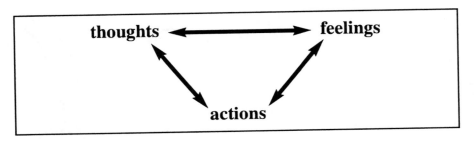

For example:

- Claire was *helping* a classmate to master a new computer programme (actions).
- Tom was *recording* in his book three targets he had recently been successful in (thoughts).
- Dean was listening to some music that always made him feel really *good and happy* (feelings).

Knowing these key principles means that we can help children experiencing depression through changing either what they think, do or feel. This means that if we can get children to think more positively about themselves this will help them. Similarly if a child helps another child in some way this can make them feel better about themselves.

As you consider some of the strategies below always remember these principles and you will be able to challenge the negative feelings a child has. Always remember to discuss your concerns with home and involve them in supporting the child as well as the child themself.

Many of these ideas you will already be using, or have already tried. Some will just not feel right. Choose those that you feel are right for you and the pupil. At times an idea that isn't right will give rise to one that is.

Being willing to offer support and showing that you care is in itself one of the best strategies.

Strategies

Positive Thinking
Because the way we think will affect how we feel, and how we feel what we think, this is an important area to work on. Depressed children will usually have negative evaluations about themselves and what happens to them. The techniques below are ideas for developing a more positive set of thoughts - thereby developing more positive feelings.

1. Rating

Ask the child on a scale of 1 to 7 to rate how they feel at specific times of the day (1 is terrible, 4 is OK and 7 is the best. If they are at 2 or 3 ask what they would need to do to move themselves to 4). Use a table to plot their scores and show signs of improvement, as shown in the diagram. It might help to use the Smiley Face Rating Scale.

M	T	W	T	F
7	7	7	7	7
6	6	6	6	6
5	5	5	5	5
4	4	4	4	4
3	3	3	3	3
2	2	2	2	2
1	1	1	1	1

Choose the face that best reflects how you are feeling.

Face 1 = 1 to 3 Things are very bad.
Face 2 = 4 & 5 I feel better now, matters are improving.
Face 3 = 6 & 7 Everything is really good.

2. Control Activities

Self-esteem involves control so involve the pupil in deciding a range of goals, help them to make decisions about their work, interests etc.

3. Target Setting

Set small targets each day and review progress. Setting a target raises self-esteem, achieving the target raises self-esteem and reflecting on their success raises self-esteem. Involve them in recording their target successes.

4. When and Will - not If and Might

Make sure that your conversations and planning sessions orient around the solution not the problem. Practise discussing what the pupil will do when they are in a positive frame of mind, then set about doing this - in small steps. Look for the improvements that will happen.

5. No more "oughts" and "shoulds"

This is challenging negative thinking. Do they think they should be top in a subject? Do they feel they should be liked by everyone? Check that their family's expectations are realistic.

6. Positive Thinking

It may seem difficult to control what we think, but it can be done. Little by little children can learn positive thoughts to think of. Thought stopping: Whenever you wish to stop what you are thinking LOOK at the big yellow board you carry in your mind which has STOP written on it and think of any three of the following and repeat them to yourself.

One thing I like about myself is ....

I look forward to ....

I feel good about ....

Something I do very well is ....

I know I can ....

One of my best qualities is ....

People like it when I ....

A recent success was when I ....

My favourite holiday was ....

People can rely on me to ....

A recent difficulty I overcame was ....

A favourite memory I have is ....

I feel good when I ....

I am at my best when I ....

A skill I have recently learned is ....

7. Evocative Words

A pupil can be encouraged to choose their own special word that they can repeat to themselves, anytime, anywhere. These words, because they are positive, will support feelings that reflect them as well as behaviours that are in tune. They can be written down for a pupil, put in code, written in touch on their back so they can recognise them. These are then repeated at set times of each day.

STRONG   HELPFUL   KIND   CARING   POSITIVE
FUNNY   SHARING   DETERMINED   POWERFUL   LOVING
SENSITIVE   SUCCESSFUL   CLEVER   IMAGINATIVE
CREATIVE   DEPENDABLE   TRUE   LOYAL   FRIENDLY
SUPPORTIVE   CHEERFUL   GENEROUS   HAPPY   PLAYFUL
PREPARED   SUNNY   TRUTHFUL   WISE   OPEN
PURPOSEFUL

8. Evocative Music

Music will also lift the spirits. If a child does not already have some music that helps them feel good, then go in search with them.

Positive Action
1. Problem Free Talk

Spend time with the pupil discussing their interests etc. What skills and qualities does this tell you about them? Can you use these skills to raise their confidence, increase their sense of value and purpose?

2. A Confidante

Depression can be in part caused through the child experiencing rejection from adults. If the pupil has an adult they get on well with and share common interests, make time to allow the relationship to develop.

3. A Brilliant Corner

Find an area of interest or skill that the pupil has and promote it. Let them teach other pupils if appropriate.

4. Social Skill Assessment

So often a pupil's depression is caused through poor peer relationships on account of their under-learned social skills. If this is the case then a programme to help them learn such skills will be needed.

5. Free Time Plan
Decide with the pupil a range of activities and places to go for each break time, where to go, what to do etc.

6. Music and Dance
Encourage the pupil to take up a social activity with exercise and music. If you can't combine all three any one or two will be beneficial. Exercise makes you feel less tired, more confident, quicker thinking and happier with others.

7. A Daily Programme
A good way to raise a pupil's self-esteem is to ensure that each day they work through a specific programme of activities that we know will be good for them.

Each Day
a) Celebrate some good news.
b) Set achievable targets.
c) Exercise.
d) Have some humour.

Positive Control
1. Control Statements
With very passive pupils provide them with a list of statements that they have to use for certain outcomes to happen. Avoid responding to their displays of inadequacy.

I need some help to complete this work.
When I finish this task can I work on the computer?
To do this task can you show me how to ...?

2. Coping
Talk with the pupil about those times when they seem to cope better. Why is that? Try to help them find the reasons and conditions that allow this and then try to plan to make it happen more often.

3. Task Review
When the pupil has completed go back over it to show them what they did and what the outcome was. What did you do to make that happen?

4. Choice - Outcome - Feedback
Set pupil a number of choices that they must make to achieve a desired goal. For example: before you can use that equipment you need to have completed at least two of the following tasks.

5. Attention
If the pupil enjoys your attention then make a point of giving it freely only when they have completed agreed tasks.

6. Positions of Responsibility
Give the pupil important tasks to do which earn them both your approval and agreed rewards.

7. Skill Development
Teach the pupil a specific skill. Record and monitor their progress to be able to show them how much they have progressed through their effort and practice. Break the skill down into small achievable steps.

8. Homework
Set the pupil the task of finding you two or three examples each day of matters improving, situations where they did something and it worked. This will help defeat negative thinking as well.

Select your strategies and place them in the record sheet and record progress on the rating scale.

INDIVIDUAL PROGRAMME PLANNER

Pupil's Name...

Date of Birth ....

Class...

Teacher/Support Staff ....

Indications of Depression/Helplessness

Long-Term Target

Short-Term Target

1. Positive Thinking Strategies

2. Positive Action Strategies

3. Positive Control Strategies

Review by Date.......................................

Remember: When you review progress with the pupil, focus on the solution and small signs of improvement.

Month Data View

EMOGRAM

Using the 7 point rating scale, involve the pupil in scoring at the end of each day how they rated it. Join the scores up to see progress at a glance. Discuss with pupil why some days are better.

M	T	W	T	F
7	7	7	7	7
6	6	6	6	6
5	5	5	5	5
4	4	4	4	4
3	3	3	3	3
2	2	2	2	2
1	1	1	1	1

M	T	W	T	F
7	7	7	7	7
6	6	6	6	6
5	5	5	5	5
4	4	4	4	4
3	3	3	3	3
2	2	2	2	2
1	1	1	1	1

M	T	W	T	F
7	7	7	7	7
6	6	6	6	6
5	5	5	5	5
4	4	4	4	4
3	3	3	3	3
2	2	2	2	2
1	1	1	1	1

M	T	W	T	F
7	7	7	7	7
6	6	6	6	6
5	5	5	5	5
4	4	4	4	4
3	3	3	3	3
2	2	2	2	2
1	1	1	1	1

Review Date ....

While there are no "quick fix" solutions the information and techniques in this booklet will enable schools to support depressed children more effectively and with greater confidence.

21

References

Blackburn, I. & Davidson. K. (1990) *Cognitive Therapy for Depression and Anxiety,* Blackwell Science: Oxford.

DfE (1994) *Code of Practice on the Identification and Assessment of Special Educational Needs,* Department for Education: London.

Graham, P. & Hughes, C. (1995) *So Young, So Sad, So Listen,* Gaskell: West London Health Promotion Agency.

Harrington, R. (1995) *Depressive Disorder in Childhood and Adolescence,* John Wiley and Sons: Chichester.

Hobday, A. & Ollier, K. (1998) *Creative therapy,* BPS Books: Leicester.

Oster, G. & Montgomery, S. (1995) *Helping Your Depressed Teenager,* John Wiley and Sons: Chichester.

Slaby, A. & Garfinkel, L. (1994) *No one saw my pain: Why teens kill themselves,* W. W. Norton and Company: New York.